THE ENTREPRENEUR'S

f6

JOURNAL

BY CLAY CLARK

Turn Your Dreams Into Reality
One Action Step and One Day at a Time

The Entrepreneur's F6 Journal
ISBN: 978-0-9984435-1-5
Copyright © 2017 by Clay Clark

Thrive Publishing

Published by Thrive Publishing
1100 Suite #100 Riverwalk Terrace
Jenks, OK 74037

Welcome to the start of your success story. Discipline is the bridge between dreams and accomplishment. Remember it's hard to build a reputation based on what you intend to do. Let's go dominate and get stuff done.

CLAY CLARK

WHO IS CLAY CLARK?

Clay is the former U.S. SBA Entrepreneur of the Year, Co-Host of the ThriveTimeShow.com Radio Show and the founder of Thrive15.com. Over the course of his career, he has been a founding team member of many successful companies including DJConnection.com, EITRLounge.com, MakeYourLifeEpic.com, Thrive15.com, and EpicPhotosTulsa.com (Dallas, Oklahoma City, etc.). He and his companies have been featured in Forbes, Fast Company, Entrepreneur, PandoDaily, Bloomberg TV, Bloomberg Radio, the Entrepreneur On Fire Podcast, the So Money Podcast with Farnoosh Torabi, and on countless media outlets. He's been the speaker of choice for Hewlett-Packard, Maytag University, O'Reilly Auto Parts, Valspar Paint, Farmers Insurance, and countless other companies. He is the father of five kids and he is the proud owner of 38 chickens, six ducks, four cats, and two Great Pyrenees dogs (at last count). Clay is an obsessive New England Patriots fan and Tim Tebow apologist. He wears a basketball jersey every day. When not chasing his kids and wife around, he enjoys reading business case studies and autobiographies about successful entrepreneurs.

NOTABLE QUOTABLES

"Rarely do we find men who willingly engage in hard, solid thinking. There is an almost universal quest for easy answers and half-baked solutions. Nothing pains some people more than having to think."

MARTIN LUTHER KING JR.
American Baptist Minister and Activist who was a leader in the Civil Rights Movement

"Thinking is the hardest work there is, which is probably the reason why so few engage in it."

HENRY FORD
American industrialist, founder of the Ford Motor Company, sponsor of the development of the assembly line technique of mass production

"Everyone needs a coach. It doesn't matter whether you're a basketball player, a tennis player, a gymnast, or a bridge player... with no feedback, no coaching, there's just no way to improve."

BILL GATES
An American business magnate, investor, author and philanthropist.

Visit **Thrive15.com** to find your business coaches and get more resources to make your business successful!

"**Success is a choice.** A choice to make trade-offs... a choice to get up early... a choice to skip lunch to hit a deadline... a choice to push through fear... a choice to work on the weekend to get ahead.... a choice to turn off the TV and open a book... a choice to hold yourself and others accountable... success is a choice that I make every day."

CLAY CLARK
Founder of Thrive15.com, former U.S. SBA Entrepreneur of the Year, host of the Thrive Time Show and America's #1 Business Coach

DAILY GOALS

Faith

time 5:30 am   duration 45 min.

Action Items: Have some quiet meditation time in the morning.

Notes: I will have to wake up earlier to have enough time.

Family

time 8:15 am / 5:45 pm   duration 15 min./3 hrs.

Action Items: Call my brother to congratulate him on the new baby. / Make a point to leave work by 5pm for family time

Notes: Ask about visiting soon. / Life runs much more smoothly if I have family time!

Finances

time 12:00 pm   duration 1 hr.

Action Items: Don't go out for lunch today, go home and make a sandwich.

Notes: I save an average of $20/wk doing this.

Friends

time 5:00 pm   duration 15 min.

Action Items: Call my best friend on the way home today and catch up on events of the week.

Notes: He's seeing someone now and seems really into her.

Fitness

time 6:30 am   duration 1 hr.

Action Items: Wreck the gym. Today is leg day.

Notes: I love leg day. I don't have to do cardio on leg day.

Fun

time 10:30 pm   duration 1/2 hr.

Action Items: Date time with the wife

Notes: Sit closer to her on the couch — that makes her happy

SCHEDULE

5:00 — Breakfast
       Meditation time
6:00 —
       Gym: Leg Day
7:00 —
       Shower
8:00 — Call Joe.

9:00 — Daily meeting with team — mention new time card rules
       Make sales calls and check in with past customers to get new deals!
10:00 —
       Work crunch time: knock out projects for PIT and Stone Lion. Move on to Slate
11:00 — if there is extra time.

12:00 — Lunch at home

1:00 — Meeting with Regan S. to discuss details of project

2:00 — Work crunch time: knock out projects for Slate, Morrison, and White Hawk. Move
       on to Ferrison project if there is extra time.
3:00 —

4:00 — Social Media Post prep and schedule for next week

5:00 — Call Aaron on the way home
       Family time:
6:00 — Ask Ashley about the school play
       Help Jennifer with the dishes after dinner — ask about her boyfriend's bball game
7:00 — Help Jonathan with accounting homework

8:00 —

9:00 — Kids to bed
       Wife time
10:00 —
       Date time with the Wife
11:00 — Bed

Sketch of the Day:

Biggest Limiting Factor:

Laziness. It's easier to sleep in, text instead of call, get fast food around the corner, and not go to the gym.

Aha! Moment:

I make a mean sandwich! And I won't feel sluggish at the gym later!

Observations:

Meditation helped me value my family and friends, eating healthy saved me money/ got me through leg day. The fun recharges and relaxes me at the end of the day! I have to focus on all 6 to make it work!

DAILY GOALS

Faith
time   duration

Action Items: _____

_____

Notes: _____

Family
time   duration

Action Items: _____

_____

Notes: _____

Finances
time   duration

Action Items: _____

_____

Notes: _____

Friends
time   duration

Action Items: _____

_____

Notes: _____

Fitness
time   duration

Action Items: _____

_____

Notes: _____

Fun
time   duration

Action Items: _____

_____

Notes: _____

SCHEDULE

5:00 —

6:00 —

7:00 —

8:00 —

9:00 —

10:00 —

11:00 —

12:00 —

1:00 —

2:00 —

3:00 —

4:00 —

5:00 —

6:00 —

7:00 —

8:00 —

9:00 —

10:00 —

11:00 —

Sketch of the Day:

Biggest Limiting Factor:

Aha! Moment:

Observations:

DAILY GOALS

Faith
time   duration

Action Items: _____

_____

Notes: _____

Family
time   duration

Action Items: _____

_____

Notes: _____

Finances
time   duration

Action Items: _____

_____

Notes: _____

Friends
time   duration

Action Items: _____

_____

Notes: _____

Fitness
time   duration

Action Items: _____

_____

Notes: _____

Fun
time   duration

Action Items: _____

_____

Notes: _____

SCHEDULE

5:00 —

6:00 —

7:00 —

8:00 —

9:00 —

10:00 —

11:00 —

12:00 —

1:00 —

2:00 —

3:00 —

4:00 —

5:00 —

6:00 —

7:00 —

8:00 —

9:00 —

10:00 —

11:00 —

Sketch of the Day:

Biggest Limiting Factor:

Aha! Moment:

Observations:

date _____

DAILY GOALS

Faith   time _____   duration _____

Action Items: _____
_____

Notes: _____

Family   time _____   duration _____

Action Items: _____
_____

Notes: _____

Finances   time _____   duration _____

Action Items: _____
_____

Notes: _____

Friends   time _____   duration _____

Action Items: _____
_____

Notes: _____

Fitness   time _____   duration _____

Action Items: _____
_____

Notes: _____

Fun   time _____   duration _____

Action Items: _____
_____

Notes: _____

SCHEDULE

5:00 —
6:00 —
7:00 —
8:00 —
9:00 —
10:00 —
11:00 —
12:00 —
1:00 —
2:00 —
3:00 —
4:00 —
5:00 —
6:00 —
7:00 —
8:00 —
9:00 —
10:00 —
11:00 —

Sketch of the Day:

Biggest Limiting Factor:

Aha! Moment:

Observations:

DAILY GOALS

Faith
time _____ duration _____

Action Items: _____

_____

Notes: _____

Family
time _____ duration _____

Action Items: _____

_____

Notes: _____

Finances
time _____ duration _____

Action Items: _____

_____

Notes: _____

Friends
time _____ duration _____

Action Items: _____

_____

Notes: _____

Fitness
time _____ duration _____

Action Items: _____

_____

Notes: _____

Fun
time _____ duration _____

Action Items: _____

_____

Notes: _____

SCHEDULE

5:00 —

6:00 —

7:00 —

8:00 —

9:00 —

10:00 —

11:00 —

12:00 —

1:00 —

2:00 —

3:00 —

4:00 —

5:00 —

6:00 —

7:00 —

8:00 —

9:00 —

10:00 —

11:00 —

Sketch of the Day: —

Biggest Limiting Factor:

Aha! Moment:

Observations:

date _____

DAILY GOALS

Faith

time _____   duration _____

Action Items: _____

_____

Notes: _____

Family

time _____   duration _____

Action Items: _____

_____

Notes: _____

Finances

time _____   duration _____

Action Items: _____

_____

Notes: _____

Friends

time _____   duration _____

Action Items: _____

_____

Notes: _____

Fitness

time _____   duration _____

Action Items: _____

_____

Notes: _____

Fun

time _____   duration _____

Action Items: _____

_____

Notes: _____

SCHEDULE

5:00 —

6:00 —

7:00 —

8:00 —

9:00 —

10:00 —

11:00 —

12:00 —

1:00 —

2:00 —

3:00 —

4:00 —

5:00 —

6:00 —

7:00 —

8:00 —

9:00 —

10:00 —

11:00 —

Sketch of the Day:

Biggest Limiting Factor:

Aha! Moment:

Observations:

date _____

DAILY GOALS

Faith   *time* _____ *duration* _____

Action Items: _____

_____

Notes: _____

Family   *time* _____ *duration* _____

Action Items: _____

_____

Notes: _____

Finances   *time* _____ *duration* _____

Action Items: _____

_____

Notes: _____

Friends   *time* _____ *duration* _____

Action Items: _____

_____

Notes: _____

Fitness   *time* _____ *duration* _____

Action Items: _____

_____

Notes: _____

Fun   *time* _____ *duration* _____

Action Items: _____

_____

Notes: _____

SCHEDULE

5:00 —

6:00 —

7:00 —

8:00 —

9:00 —

10:00 —

11:00 —

12:00 —

1:00 —

2:00 —

3:00 —

4:00 —

5:00 —

6:00 —

7:00 —

8:00 —

9:00 —

10:00 —

11:00 —

Sketch of the Day:

Biggest Limiting Factor:

Aha! Moment:

Observations:

DAILY GOALS

Faith
time _____ duration _____

Action Items: _____

_____

Notes: _____

Family
time _____ duration _____

Action Items: _____

_____

Notes: _____

Finances
time _____ duration _____

Action Items: _____

_____

Notes: _____

Friends
time _____ duration _____

Action Items: _____

_____

Notes: _____

Fitness
time _____ duration _____

Action Items: _____

_____

Notes: _____

Fun
time _____ duration _____

Action Items: _____

_____

Notes: _____

SCHEDULE

5:00 —

6:00 —

7:00 —

8:00 —

9:00 —

10:00 —

11:00 —

12:00 —

1:00 —

2:00 —

3:00 —

4:00 —

5:00 —

6:00 —

7:00 —

8:00 —

9:00 —

10:00 —

11:00 —

Sketch of the Day:

Biggest Limiting Factor:

Aha! Moment:

Observations:

date _____

DAILY GOALS

Faith
time   duration

Action Items: _____

_____

Notes: _____

Family
time   duration

Action Items: _____

_____

Notes: _____

Finances
time   duration

Action Items: _____

_____

Notes: _____

Friends
time   duration

Action Items: _____

_____

Notes: _____

Fitness
time   duration

Action Items: _____

_____

Notes: _____

Fun
time   duration

Action Items: _____

_____

Notes: _____

SCHEDULE

5:00 —

6:00 —

7:00 —

8:00 —

9:00 —

10:00 —

11:00 —

12:00 —

1:00 —

2:00 —

3:00 —

4:00 —

5:00 —

6:00 —

7:00 —

8:00 —

9:00 —

10:00 —

11:00 —

Sketch of the Day:

Biggest Limiting Factor:

Aha! Moment:

Observations:

DAILY GOALS

Faith

time _____ duration _____

Action Items: _____

_____

Notes: _____

Family

time _____ duration _____

Action Items: _____

_____

Notes: _____

Finances

time _____ duration _____

Action Items: _____

_____

Notes: _____

Friends

time _____ duration _____

Action Items: _____

_____

Notes: _____

Fitness

time _____ duration _____

Action Items: _____

_____

Notes: _____

Fun

time _____ duration _____

Action Items: _____

_____

Notes: _____

SCHEDULE

5:00 —

6:00 —

7:00 —

8:00 —

9:00 —

10:00 —

11:00 —

12:00 —

1:00 —

2:00 —

3:00 —

4:00 —

5:00 —

6:00 —

7:00 —

8:00 —

9:00 —

10:00 —

11:00 —

Sketch of the Day:

Biggest Limiting Factor:

Aha! Moment:

Observations:

date _____

DAILY GOALS

Faith   time _____   duration _____

Action Items: _____

_____

Notes: _____

Family   time _____   duration _____

Action Items: _____

_____

Notes: _____

Finances   time _____   duration _____

Action Items: _____

_____

Notes: _____

Friends   time _____   duration _____

Action Items: _____

_____

Notes: _____

Fitness   time _____   duration _____

Action Items: _____

_____

Notes: _____

Fun   time _____   duration _____

Action Items: _____

_____

Notes: _____

SCHEDULE

5:00 —

6:00 —

7:00 —

8:00 —

9:00 —

10:00 —

11:00 —

12:00 —

1:00 —

2:00 —

3:00 —

4:00 —

5:00 —

6:00 —

7:00 —

8:00 —

9:00 —

10:00 —

11:00 —

Sketch of the Day:

Biggest Limiting Factor:

Aha! Moment:

Observations:

DAILY GOALS

Faith

time   duration

Action Items: _____

_____

Notes: _____

Family

time   duration

Action Items: _____

_____

Notes: _____

Finances

time   duration

Action Items: _____

_____

Notes: _____

Friends

time   duration

Action Items: _____

_____

Notes: _____

Fitness

time   duration

Action Items: _____

_____

Notes: _____

Fun

time   duration

Action Items: _____

_____

Notes: _____

SCHEDULE

5:00 —

6:00 —

7:00 —

8:00 —

9:00 —

10:00 —

11:00 —

12:00 —

1:00 —

2:00 —

3:00 —

4:00 —

5:00 —

6:00 —

7:00 —

8:00 —

9:00 —

10:00 —

11:00 —

Sketch of the Day:

Biggest Limiting Factor:

Aha! Moment:

Observations:

DAILY GOALS

Faith
time   duration

Action Items: _____

_____

Notes: _____

Family
time   duration

Action Items: _____

_____

Notes: _____

Finances
time   duration

Action Items: _____

_____

Notes: _____

Friends
time   duration

Action Items: _____

_____

Notes: _____

Fitness
time   duration

Action Items: _____

_____

Notes: _____

Fun
time   duration

Action Items: _____

_____

Notes: _____

SCHEDULE

5:00 —

6:00 —

7:00 —

8:00 —

9:00 —

10:00 —

11:00 —

12:00 —

1:00 —

2:00 —

3:00 —

4:00 —

5:00 —

6:00 —

7:00 —

8:00 —

9:00 —

10:00 —

11:00 —

Sketch of the Day:

Biggest Limiting Factor:

Aha! Moment:

Observations:

DAILY GOALS

Faith

time _____ duration _____

Action Items: _____

_____

Notes: _____

Family

time _____ duration _____

Action Items: _____

_____

Notes: _____

Finances

time _____ duration _____

Action Items: _____

_____

Notes: _____

Friends

time _____ duration _____

Action Items: _____

_____

Notes: _____

Fitness

time _____ duration _____

Action Items: _____

_____

Notes: _____

Fun

time _____ duration _____

Action Items: _____

_____

Notes: _____

SCHEDULE

5:00 —

6:00 —

7:00 —

8:00 —

9:00 —

10:00 —

11:00 —

12:00 —

1:00 —

2:00 —

3:00 —

4:00 —

5:00 —

6:00 —

7:00 —

8:00 —

9:00 —

10:00 —

11:00 —

Sketch of the Day:

Biggest Limiting Factor:

Aha! Moment:

Observations:

date ______________

DAILY GOALS

Faith
time duration

Action Items:

Notes:

Family
time duration

Action Items:

Notes:

Finances
time duration

Action Items:

Notes:

Friends
time duration

Action Items:

Notes:

Fitness
time duration

Action Items:

Notes:

Fun
time duration

Action Items:

Notes:

SCHEDULE

5:00 —

6:00 —

7:00 —

8:00 —

9:00 —

10:00 —

11:00 —

12:00 —

1:00 —

2:00 —

3:00 —

4:00 —

5:00 —

6:00 —

7:00 —

8:00 —

9:00 —

10:00 —

11:00 —

Sketch of the Day:

Biggest Limiting Factor:

Aha! Moment:

Observations:

date _____

DAILY GOALS

Faith time _____ duration _____

Action Items: _____

_____

Notes: _____

Family time _____ duration _____

Action Items: _____

_____

Notes: _____

Finances time _____ duration _____

Action Items: _____

_____

Notes: _____

Friends time _____ duration _____

Action Items: _____

_____

Notes: _____

Fitness time _____ duration _____

Action Items: _____

_____

Notes: _____

Fun time _____ duration _____

Action Items: _____

_____

Notes: _____

SCHEDULE

5:00 —

6:00 —

7:00 —

8:00 —

9:00 —

10:00 —

11:00 —

12:00 —

1:00 —

2:00 —

3:00 —

4:00 —

5:00 —

6:00 —

7:00 —

8:00 —

9:00 —

10:00 —

11:00 —

Sketch of the Day:

Biggest Limiting Factor:

Aha! Moment:

Observations:

DAILY GOALS

Faith

time _____ duration _____

Action Items: _____

_____

Notes: _____

Family

time _____ duration _____

Action Items: _____

_____

Notes: _____

Finances

time _____ duration _____

Action Items: _____

_____

Notes: _____

Friends

time _____ duration _____

Action Items: _____

_____

Notes: _____

Fitness

time _____ duration _____

Action Items: _____

_____

Notes: _____

Fun

time _____ duration _____

Action Items: _____

_____

Notes: _____

SCHEDULE

5:00 —

6:00 —

7:00 —

8:00 —

9:00 —

10:00 —

11:00 —

12:00 —

1:00 —

2:00 —

3:00 —

4:00 —

5:00 —

6:00 —

7:00 —

8:00 —

9:00 —

10:00 —

11:00 —

Sketch of the Day:

Biggest Limiting Factor:

Aha! Moment:

Observations:

date _____

DAILY GOALS

Faith
time _____ duration _____

Action Items: _____

_____

Notes: _____

Family
time _____ duration _____

Action Items: _____

_____

Notes: _____

Finances
time _____ duration _____

Action Items: _____

_____

Notes: _____

Friends
time _____ duration _____

Action Items: _____

_____

Notes: _____

Fitness
time _____ duration _____

Action Items: _____

_____

Notes: _____

Fun
time _____ duration _____

Action Items: _____

_____

Notes: _____

SCHEDULE

5:00 —

6:00 —

7:00 —

8:00 —

9:00 —

10:00 —

11:00 —

12:00 —

1:00 —

2:00 —

3:00 —

4:00 —

5:00 —

6:00 —

7:00 —

8:00 —

9:00 —

10:00 —

11:00 —

Sketch of the Day:

Biggest Limiting Factor:

Aha! Moment:

Observations:

DAILY GOALS

Faith
time   *duration*

Action Items: _____

_____

Notes: _____

Family
time   *duration*

Action Items: _____

_____

Notes: _____

Finances
time   *duration*

Action Items: _____

_____

Notes: _____

Friends
time   *duration*

Action Items: _____

_____

Notes: _____

Fitness
time   *duration*

Action Items: _____

_____

Notes: _____

Fun
time   *duration*

Action Items: _____

_____

Notes: _____

SCHEDULE

5:00 —

6:00 —

7:00 —

8:00 —

9:00 —

10:00 —

11:00 —

12:00 —

1:00 —

2:00 —

3:00 —

4:00 —

5:00 —

6:00 —

7:00 —

8:00 —

9:00 —

10:00 —

11:00 —

Sketch of the Day:

Biggest Limiting Factor:

Aha! Moment:

Observations:

date _____

DAILY GOALS

Faith
time _____ duration _____

Action Items: _____

_____

Notes: _____

Family
time _____ duration _____

Action Items: _____

_____

Notes: _____

Finances
time _____ duration _____

Action Items: _____

_____

Notes: _____

Friends
time _____ duration _____

Action Items: _____

_____

Notes: _____

Fitness
time _____ duration _____

Action Items: _____

_____

Notes: _____

Fun
time _____ duration _____

Action Items: _____

_____

Notes: _____

SCHEDULE

5:00 —

6:00 —

7:00 —

8:00 —

9:00 —

10:00 —

11:00 —

12:00 —

1:00 —

2:00 —

3:00 —

4:00 —

5:00 —

6:00 —

7:00 —

8:00 —

9:00 —

10:00 —

11:00 —

Sketch of the Day:

Biggest Limiting Factor:

Aha! Moment:

Observations:

DAILY GOALS

Faith
time　　　　　　　duration

Action Items: _____

_____

Notes: _____

Family
time　　　　　　　duration

Action Items: _____

_____

Notes: _____

Finances
time　　　　　　　duration

Action Items: _____

_____

Notes: _____

Friends
time　　　　　　　duration

Action Items: _____

_____

Notes: _____

Fitness
time　　　　　　　duration

Action Items: _____

_____

Notes: _____

Fun
time　　　　　　　duration

Action Items: _____

_____

Notes: _____

SCHEDULE

5:00 —

6:00 —

7:00 —

8:00 —

9:00 —

10:00 —

11:00 —

12:00 —

1:00 —

2:00 —

3:00 —

4:00 —

5:00 —

6:00 —

7:00 —

8:00 —

9:00 —

10:00 —

11:00 —

Sketch of the Day:

Biggest Limiting Factor:

Aha! Moment:

Observations:

date _____

DAILY GOALS

Faith   time [   ]   duration [   ]

Action Items: _____

_____

Notes: _____

Family   time [   ]   duration [   ]

Action Items: _____

_____

Notes: _____

Finances   time [   ]   duration [   ]

Action Items: _____

_____

Notes: _____

Friends   time [   ]   duration [   ]

Action Items: _____

_____

Notes: _____

Fitness   time [   ]   duration [   ]

Action Items: _____

_____

Notes: _____

Fun   time [   ]   duration [   ]

Action Items: _____

_____

Notes: _____

SCHEDULE

5:00 —

6:00 —

7:00 —

8:00 —

9:00 —

10:00 —

11:00 —

12:00 —

1:00 —

2:00 —

3:00 —

4:00 —

5:00 —

6:00 —

7:00 —

8:00 —

9:00 —

10:00 —

11:00 —

Sketch of the Day:

Biggest Limiting Factor:

Aha! Moment:

Observations:

DAILY GOALS

Faith
time _____ duration _____
Action Items: _____

_____
Notes: _____

Family
time _____ duration _____
Action Items: _____

_____
Notes: _____

Finances
time _____ duration _____
Action Items: _____

_____
Notes: _____

Friends
time _____ duration _____
Action Items: _____

_____
Notes: _____

Fitness
time _____ duration _____
Action Items: _____

_____
Notes: _____

Fun
time _____ duration _____
Action Items: _____

_____
Notes: _____

SCHEDULE

5:00 —

6:00 —

7:00 —

8:00 —

9:00 —

10:00 —

11:00 —

12:00 —

1:00 —

2:00 —

3:00 —

4:00 —

5:00 —

6:00 —

7:00 —

8:00 —

9:00 —

10:00 —

11:00 —

Sketch of the Day:

Biggest Limiting Factor:

Aha! Moment:

Observations:

DAILY GOALS

Faith

time   duration

Action Items: _____

_____

Notes: _____

Family

time   duration

Action Items: _____

_____

Notes: _____

Finances

time   duration

Action Items: _____

_____

Notes: _____

Friends

time   duration

Action Items: _____

_____

Notes: _____

Fitness

time   duration

Action Items: _____

_____

Notes: _____

Fun

time   duration

Action Items: _____

_____

Notes: _____

SCHEDULE

5:00 —
6:00 —
7:00 —
8:00 —
9:00 —
10:00 —
11:00 —
12:00 —
1:00 —
2:00 —
3:00 —
4:00 —
5:00 —
6:00 —
7:00 —
8:00 —
9:00 —
10:00 —
11:00 —

Sketch of the Day:

Biggest Limiting Factor:

Aha! Moment:

Observations:

date _____

DAILY GOALS

Faith
time _____ duration _____

Action Items: _____

_____

Notes: _____

Family
time _____ duration _____

Action Items: _____

_____

Notes: _____

Finances
time _____ duration _____

Action Items: _____

_____

Notes: _____

Friends
time _____ duration _____

Action Items: _____

_____

Notes: _____

Fitness
time _____ duration _____

Action Items: _____

_____

Notes: _____

Fun
time _____ duration _____

Action Items: _____

_____

Notes: _____

SCHEDULE

5:00 —

6:00 —

7:00 —

8:00 —

9:00 —

10:00 —

11:00 —

12:00 —

1:00 —

2:00 —

3:00 —

4:00 —

5:00 —

6:00 —

7:00 —

8:00 —

9:00 —

10:00 —

11:00 —

Sketch of the Day:

Biggest Limiting Factor:

Aha! Moment:

Observations:

date _____

DAILY GOALS

Faith
time _____ duration _____

Action Items: _____

_____

Notes: _____

Family
time _____ duration _____

Action Items: _____

_____

Notes: _____

Finances
time _____ duration _____

Action Items: _____

_____

Notes: _____

Friends
time _____ duration _____

Action Items: _____

_____

Notes: _____

Fitness
time _____ duration _____

Action Items: _____

_____

Notes: _____

Fun
time _____ duration _____

Action Items: _____

_____

Notes: _____

SCHEDULE

5:00 —

6:00 —

7:00 —

8:00 —

9:00 —

10:00 —

11:00 —

12:00 —

1:00 —

2:00 —

3:00 —

4:00 —

5:00 —

6:00 —

7:00 —

8:00 —

9:00 —

10:00 —

11:00 —

Sketch of the Day:

Biggest Limiting Factor:

Aha! Moment:

Observations:

DAILY GOALS

Faith

time   duration

Action Items: _____

_____

Notes: _____

Family

time   duration

Action Items: _____

_____

Notes: _____

Finances

time   duration

Action Items: _____

_____

Notes: _____

Friends

time   duration

Action Items: _____

_____

Notes: _____

Fitness

time   duration

Action Items: _____

_____

Notes: _____

Fun

time   duration

Action Items: _____

_____

Notes: _____

SCHEDULE

5:00 —

6:00 —

7:00 —

8:00 —

9:00 —

10:00 —

11:00 —

12:00 —

1:00 —

2:00 —

3:00 —

4:00 —

5:00 —

6:00 —

7:00 —

8:00 —

9:00 —

10:00 —

11:00 —

Sketch of the Day:

Biggest Limiting Factor:

Aha! Moment:

Observations:

date _____

DAILY GOALS

Faith
time   duration

Action Items: _____

_____

Notes: _____

Family
time   duration

Action Items: _____

_____

Notes: _____

Finances
time   duration

Action Items: _____

_____

Notes: _____

Friends
time   duration

Action Items: _____

_____

Notes: _____

Fitness
time   duration

Action Items: _____

_____

Notes: _____

Fun
time   duration

Action Items: _____

_____

Notes: _____

SCHEDULE

5:00 —
6:00 —
7:00 —
8:00 —
9:00 —
10:00 —
11:00 —
12:00 —
1:00 —
2:00 —
3:00 —
4:00 —
5:00 —
6:00 —
7:00 —
8:00 —
9:00 —
10:00 —
11:00 —

Sketch of the Day:

Biggest Limiting Factor:

Aha! Moment:

Observations:

DAILY GOALS

Faith
time ▓▓▓▓▓▓▓ duration ▓▓▓▓▓▓▓

Action Items: _____

_____

Notes: _____

Family
time ▓▓▓▓▓▓▓ duration ▓▓▓▓▓▓▓

Action Items: _____

_____

Notes: _____

Finances
time ▓▓▓▓▓▓▓ duration ▓▓▓▓▓▓▓

Action Items: _____

_____

Notes: _____

Friends
time ▓▓▓▓▓▓▓ duration ▓▓▓▓▓▓▓

Action Items: _____

_____

Notes: _____

Fitness
time ▓▓▓▓▓▓▓ duration ▓▓▓▓▓▓▓

Action Items: _____

_____

Notes: _____

Fun
time ▓▓▓▓▓▓▓ duration ▓▓▓▓▓▓▓

Action Items: _____

_____

Notes: _____

SCHEDULE

5:00 —

6:00 —

7:00 —

8:00 —

9:00 —

10:00 —

11:00 —

12:00 —

1:00 —

2:00 —

3:00 —

4:00 —

5:00 —

6:00 —

7:00 —

8:00 —

9:00 —

10:00 —

11:00 —

Sketch of the Day:

Biggest Limiting Factor:

Aha! Moment:

Observations:

date _____

DAILY GOALS

Faith
time _____ duration _____

Action Items: _____

_____

Notes: _____

Family
time _____ duration _____

Action Items: _____

_____

Notes: _____

Finances
time _____ duration _____

Action Items: _____

_____

Notes: _____

Friends
time _____ duration _____

Action Items: _____

_____

Notes: _____

Fitness
time _____ duration _____

Action Items: _____

_____

Notes: _____

Fun
time _____ duration _____

Action Items: _____

_____

Notes: _____

SCHEDULE

5:00 —

6:00 —

7:00 —

8:00 —

9:00 —

10:00 —

11:00 —

12:00 —

1:00 —

2:00 —

3:00 —

4:00 —

5:00 —

6:00 —

7:00 —

8:00 —

9:00 —

10:00 —

11:00 —

Sketch of the Day:

Biggest Limiting Factor:

Aha! Moment:

Observations:

date _____

DAILY GOALS

Faith   time _____   duration _____

Action Items: _____

_____

Notes: _____

Family   time _____   duration _____

Action Items: _____

_____

Notes: _____

Finances   time _____   duration _____

Action Items: _____

_____

Notes: _____

Friends   time _____   duration _____

Action Items: _____

_____

Notes: _____

Fitness   time _____   duration _____

Action Items: _____

_____

Notes: _____

Fun   time _____   duration _____

Action Items: _____

_____

Notes: _____

SCHEDULE

5:00 —
6:00 —
7:00 —
8:00 —
9:00 —
10:00 —
11:00 —
12:00 —
1:00 —
2:00 —
3:00 —
4:00 —
5:00 —
6:00 —
7:00 —
8:00 —
9:00 —
10:00 —
11:00 —

Sketch of the Day:

Biggest Limiting Factor:

Aha! Moment:

Observations:

date _____

DAILY GOALS

Faith
time _____ duration _____

Action Items: _____

_____

Notes: _____

Family
time _____ duration _____

Action Items: _____

_____

Notes: _____

Finances
time _____ duration _____

Action Items: _____

_____

Notes: _____

Friends
time _____ duration _____

Action Items: _____

_____

Notes: _____

Fitness
time _____ duration _____

Action Items: _____

_____

Notes: _____

Fun
time _____ duration _____

Action Items: _____

_____

Notes: _____

SCHEDULE

5:00 —

6:00 —

7:00 —

8:00 —

9:00 —

10:00 —

11:00 —

12:00 —

1:00 —

2:00 —

3:00 —

4:00 —

5:00 —

6:00 —

7:00 —

8:00 —

9:00 —

10:00 —

11:00 —

Sketch of the Day:

Biggest Limiting Factor:

Aha! Moment:

Observations:

date _____

DAILY GOALS

Faith   *time* _____   *duration* _____

Action Items: _____

_____

Notes: _____

Family   *time* _____   *duration* _____

Action Items: _____

_____

Notes: _____

Finances   *time* _____   *duration* _____

Action Items: _____

_____

Notes: _____

Friends   *time* _____   *duration* _____

Action Items: _____

_____

Notes: _____

Fitness   *time* _____   *duration* _____

Action Items: _____

_____

Notes: _____

Fun   *time* _____   *duration* _____

Action Items: _____

_____

Notes: _____

SCHEDULE

5:00 —

6:00 —

7:00 —

8:00 —

9:00 —

10:00 —

11:00 —

12:00 —

1:00 —

2:00 —

3:00 —

4:00 —

5:00 —

6:00 —

7:00 —

8:00 —

9:00 —

10:00 —

11:00 —

Sketch of the Day:

Biggest Limiting Factor:

Aha! Moment:

Observations:

DAILY GOALS

Faith

time _____ duration _____

Action Items: _____

_____

Notes: _____

Family

time _____ duration _____

Action Items: _____

_____

Notes: _____

Finances

time _____ duration _____

Action Items: _____

_____

Notes: _____

Friends

time _____ duration _____

Action Items: _____

_____

Notes: _____

Fitness

time _____ duration _____

Action Items: _____

_____

Notes: _____

Fun

time _____ duration _____

Action Items: _____

_____

Notes: _____

SCHEDULE

5:00 —

6:00 —

7:00 —

8:00 —

9:00 —

10:00 —

11:00 —

12:00 —

1:00 —

2:00 —

3:00 —

4:00 —

5:00 —

6:00 —

7:00 —

8:00 —

9:00 —

10:00 —

11:00 —

Sketch of the Day:

Biggest Limiting Factor:

Aha! Moment:

Observations:

date _____

DAILY GOALS

Faith   time _____   duration _____

Action Items: _____

_____

Notes: _____

Family   time _____   duration _____

Action Items: _____

_____

Notes: _____

Finances   time _____   duration _____

Action Items: _____

_____

Notes: _____

Friends   time _____   duration _____

Action Items: _____

_____

Notes: _____

Fitness   time _____   duration _____

Action Items: _____

_____

Notes: _____

Fun   time _____   duration _____

Action Items: _____

_____

Notes: _____

SCHEDULE

5:00 —

6:00 —

7:00 —

8:00 —

9:00 —

10:00 —

11:00 —

12:00 —

1:00 —

2:00 —

3:00 —

4:00 —

5:00 —

6:00 —

7:00 —

8:00 —

9:00 —

10:00 —

11:00 —

Sketch of the Day:

Biggest Limiting Factor:

Aha! Moment:

Observations:

date _____

DAILY GOALS

Faith
time _____ duration _____

Action Items: _____

_____

Notes: _____

Family
time _____ duration _____

Action Items: _____

_____

Notes: _____

Finances
time _____ duration _____

Action Items: _____

_____

Notes: _____

Friends
time _____ duration _____

Action Items: _____

_____

Notes: _____

Fitness
time _____ duration _____

Action Items: _____

_____

Notes: _____

Fun
time _____ duration _____

Action Items: _____

_____

Notes: _____

SCHEDULE

5:00 —

6:00 —

7:00 —

8:00 —

9:00 —

10:00 —

11:00 —

12:00 —

1:00 —

2:00 —

3:00 —

4:00 —

5:00 —

6:00 —

7:00 —

8:00 —

9:00 —

10:00 —

11:00 —

Sketch of the Day:

Biggest Limiting Factor:

Aha! Moment:

Observations:

date _____

DAILY GOALS

Faith   time _____   duration _____

Action Items: _____

_____

Notes: _____

Family   time _____   duration _____

Action Items: _____

_____

Notes: _____

Finances   time _____   duration _____

Action Items: _____

_____

Notes: _____

Friends   time _____   duration _____

Action Items: _____

_____

Notes: _____

Fitness   time _____   duration _____

Action Items: _____

_____

Notes: _____

Fun   time _____   duration _____

Action Items: _____

_____

Notes: _____

SCHEDULE

5:00 —

6:00 —

7:00 —

8:00 —

9:00 —

10:00 —

11:00 —

12:00 —

1:00 —

2:00 —

3:00 —

4:00 —

5:00 —

6:00 —

7:00 —

8:00 —

9:00 —

10:00 —

11:00 —

Sketch of the Day:

Biggest Limiting Factor:

Aha! Moment:

Observations:

date _____

DAILY GOALS

Faith
time   duration

Action Items: _____

_____

Notes: _____

Family
time   duration

Action Items: _____

_____

Notes: _____

Finances
time   duration

Action Items: _____

_____

Notes: _____

Friends
time   duration

Action Items: _____

_____

Notes: _____

Fitness
time   duration

Action Items: _____

_____

Notes: _____

Fun
time   duration

Action Items: _____

_____

Notes: _____

SCHEDULE

5:00 —

6:00 —

7:00 —

8:00 —

9:00 —

10:00 —

11:00 —

12:00 —

1:00 —

2:00 —

3:00 —

4:00 —

5:00 —

6:00 —

7:00 —

8:00 —

9:00 —

10:00 —

11:00 —

Sketch of the Day:

Biggest Limiting Factor:

Aha! Moment:

Observations:

date _____

DAILY GOALS

Faith
time _____ duration _____
Action Items: _____
_____
Notes: _____

Family
time _____ duration _____
Action Items: _____
_____
Notes: _____

Finances
time _____ duration _____
Action Items: _____
_____
Notes: _____

Friends
time _____ duration _____
Action Items: _____
_____
Notes: _____

Fitness
time _____ duration _____
Action Items: _____
_____
Notes: _____

Fun
time _____ duration _____
Action Items: _____
_____
Notes: _____

SCHEDULE

5:00 —

6:00 —

7:00 —

8:00 —

9:00 —

10:00 —

11:00 —

12:00 —

1:00 —

2:00 —

3:00 —

4:00 —

5:00 —

6:00 —

7:00 —

8:00 —

9:00 —

10:00 —

11:00 —

Sketch of the Day:

Biggest Limiting Factor:

Aha! Moment:

Observations:

DAILY GOALS

Faith
time _____ duration _____

Action Items: _____

_____

Notes: _____

Family
time _____ duration _____

Action Items: _____

_____

Notes: _____

Finances
time _____ duration _____

Action Items: _____

_____

Notes: _____

Friends
time _____ duration _____

Action Items: _____

_____

Notes: _____

Fitness
time _____ duration _____

Action Items: _____

_____

Notes: _____

Fun
time _____ duration _____

Action Items: _____

_____

Notes: _____

SCHEDULE

5:00 —

6:00 —

7:00 —

8:00 —

9:00 —

10:00 —

11:00 —

12:00 —

1:00 —

2:00 —

3:00 —

4:00 —

5:00 —

6:00 —

7:00 —

8:00 —

9:00 —

10:00 —

11:00 —

Sketch of the Day: ⎯⎯⎯⎯⎯⎯⎯

Biggest Limiting Factor:

Aha! Moment:

Observations:

DAILY GOALS

Faith
time _____ duration _____

Action Items: _____

_____

Notes: _____

Family
time _____ duration _____

Action Items: _____

_____

Notes: _____

Finances
time _____ duration _____

Action Items: _____

_____

Notes: _____

Friends
time _____ duration _____

Action Items: _____

_____

Notes: _____

Fitness
time _____ duration _____

Action Items: _____

_____

Notes: _____

Fun
time _____ duration _____

Action Items: _____

_____

Notes: _____

SCHEDULE

5:00 —

6:00 —

7:00 —

8:00 —

9:00 —

10:00 —

11:00 —

12:00 —

1:00 —

2:00 —

3:00 —

4:00 —

5:00 —

6:00 —

7:00 —

8:00 —

9:00 —

10:00 —

11:00 —

Sketch of the Day:

Biggest Limiting Factor:

Aha! Moment:

Observations:

DAILY GOALS

Faith
time _____   duration _____

Action Items: _____

_____

Notes: _____

Family
time _____   duration _____

Action Items: _____

_____

Notes: _____

Finances
time _____   duration _____

Action Items: _____

_____

Notes: _____

Friends
time _____   duration _____

Action Items: _____

_____

Notes: _____

Fitness
time _____   duration _____

Action Items: _____

_____

Notes: _____

Fun
time _____   duration _____

Action Items: _____

_____

Notes: _____

SCHEDULE

5:00 —

6:00 —

7:00 —

8:00 —

9:00 —

10:00 —

11:00 —

12:00 —

1:00 —

2:00 —

3:00 —

4:00 —

5:00 —

6:00 —

7:00 —

8:00 —

9:00 —

10:00 —

11:00 —

Sketch of the Day:

Biggest Limiting Factor:

Aha! Moment:

Observations:

date _____

DAILY GOALS

Faith   time _____   duration _____

Action Items: _____

_____

Notes: _____

Family   time _____   duration _____

Action Items: _____

_____

Notes: _____

Finances   time _____   duration _____

Action Items: _____

_____

Notes: _____

Friends   time _____   duration _____

Action Items: _____

_____

Notes: _____

Fitness   time _____   duration _____

Action Items: _____

_____

Notes: _____

Fun   time _____   duration _____

Action Items: _____

_____

Notes: _____

SCHEDULE

5:00 —

6:00 —

7:00 —

8:00 —

9:00 —

10:00 —

11:00 —

12:00 —

1:00 —

2:00 —

3:00 —

4:00 —

5:00 —

6:00 —

7:00 —

8:00 —

9:00 —

10:00 —

11:00 —

Sketch of the Day:

Biggest Limiting Factor:

Aha! Moment:

Observations:

DAILY GOALS

Faith
time _____ duration _____

Action Items: _____

_____

Notes: _____

Family
time _____ duration _____

Action Items: _____

_____

Notes: _____

Finances
time _____ duration _____

Action Items: _____

_____

Notes: _____

Friends
time _____ duration _____

Action Items: _____

_____

Notes: _____

Fitness
time _____ duration _____

Action Items: _____

_____

Notes: _____

Fun
time _____ duration _____

Action Items: _____

_____

Notes: _____

SCHEDULE

5:00 —

6:00 —

7:00 —

8:00 —

9:00 —

10:00 —

11:00 —

12:00 —

1:00 —

2:00 —

3:00 —

4:00 —

5:00 —

6:00 —

7:00 —

8:00 —

9:00 —

10:00 —

11:00 —

Sketch of the Day:

Biggest Limiting Factor:

Aha! Moment:

Observations:

DAILY GOALS

Faith
time _____ duration _____

Action Items: _____

_____

Notes: _____

Family
time _____ duration _____

Action Items: _____

_____

Notes: _____

Finances
time _____ duration _____

Action Items: _____

_____

Notes: _____

Friends
time _____ duration _____

Action Items: _____

_____

Notes: _____

Fitness
time _____ duration _____

Action Items: _____

_____

Notes: _____

Fun
time _____ duration _____

Action Items: _____

_____

Notes: _____

SCHEDULE

5:00 —

6:00 —

7:00 —

8:00 —

9:00 —

10:00 —

11:00 —

12:00 —

1:00 —

2:00 —

3:00 —

4:00 —

5:00 —

6:00 —

7:00 —

8:00 —

9:00 —

10:00 —

11:00 —

Sketch of the Day:

Biggest Limiting Factor:

Aha! Moment:

Observations:

date _____

DAILY GOALS

Faith
time _____ duration _____

Action Items: _____

_____

Notes: _____

Family
time _____ duration _____

Action Items: _____

_____

Notes: _____

Finances
time _____ duration _____

Action Items: _____

_____

Notes: _____

Friends
time _____ duration _____

Action Items: _____

_____

Notes: _____

Fitness
time _____ duration _____

Action Items: _____

_____

Notes: _____

Fun
time _____ duration _____

Action Items: _____

_____

Notes: _____

SCHEDULE

5:00 —

6:00 —

7:00 —

8:00 —

9:00 —

10:00 —

11:00 —

12:00 —

1:00 —

2:00 —

3:00 —

4:00 —

5:00 —

6:00 —

7:00 —

8:00 —

9:00 —

10:00 —

11:00 —

Sketch of the Day:

Biggest Limiting Factor:

Aha! Moment:

Observations:

date _____

DAILY GOALS

Faith

time ▨▨▨▨▨   duration ▨▨▨▨▨

Action Items: _____

_____

Notes: _____

Family

time ▨▨▨▨▨   duration ▨▨▨▨▨

Action Items: _____

_____

Notes: _____

Finances

time ▨▨▨▨▨   duration ▨▨▨▨▨

Action Items: _____

_____

Notes: _____

Friends

time ▨▨▨▨▨   duration ▨▨▨▨▨

Action Items: _____

_____

Notes: _____

Fitness

time ▨▨▨▨▨   duration ▨▨▨▨▨

Action Items: _____

_____

Notes: _____

Fun

time ▨▨▨▨▨   duration ▨▨▨▨▨

Action Items: _____

_____

Notes: _____

SCHEDULE

5:00 —

6:00 —

7:00 —

8:00 —

9:00 —

10:00 —

11:00 —

12:00 —

1:00 —

2:00 —

3:00 —

4:00 —

5:00 —

6:00 —

7:00 —

8:00 —

9:00 —

10:00 —

11:00 —

Sketch of the Day:

Biggest Limiting Factor:

Aha! Moment:

Observations:

date _____

DAILY GOALS

Faith
time _____ duration _____
Action Items: _____
_____
Notes: _____

Family
time _____ duration _____
Action Items: _____
_____
Notes: _____

Finances
time _____ duration _____
Action Items: _____
_____
Notes: _____

Friends
time _____ duration _____
Action Items: _____
_____
Notes: _____

Fitness
time _____ duration _____
Action Items: _____
_____
Notes: _____

Fun
time _____ duration _____
Action Items: _____
_____
Notes: _____

SCHEDULE

5:00 —

6:00 —

7:00 —

8:00 —

9:00 —

10:00 —

11:00 —

12:00 —

1:00 —

2:00 —

3:00 —

4:00 —

5:00 —

6:00 —

7:00 —

8:00 —

9:00 —

10:00 —

11:00 —

Sketch of the Day:

Biggest Limiting Factor:

Aha! Moment:

Observations:

DAILY GOALS

Faith
time duration

Action Items: _____

_____

Notes: _____

Family
time duration

Action Items: _____

_____

Notes: _____

Finances
time duration

Action Items: _____

_____

Notes: _____

Friends
time duration

Action Items: _____

_____

Notes: _____

Fitness
time duration

Action Items: _____

_____

Notes: _____

Fun
time duration

Action Items: _____

_____

Notes: _____

SCHEDULE

5:00 —

6:00 —

7:00 —

8:00 —

9:00 —

10:00 —

11:00 —

12:00 —

1:00 —

2:00 —

3:00 —

4:00 —

5:00 —

6:00 —

7:00 —

8:00 —

9:00 —

10:00 —

11:00 —

Sketch of the Day:

Biggest Limiting Factor:

Aha! Moment:

Observations:

date

DAILY GOALS

Faith
time duration

Action Items:

Notes:

Family
time duration

Action Items:

Notes:

Finances
time duration

Action Items:

Notes:

Friends
time duration

Action Items:

Notes:

Fitness
time duration

Action Items:

Notes:

Fun
time duration

Action Items:

Notes:

SCHEDULE

5:00 —

6:00 —

7:00 —

8:00 —

9:00 —

10:00 —

11:00 —

12:00 —

1:00 —

2:00 —

3:00 —

4:00 —

5:00 —

6:00 —

7:00 —

8:00 —

9:00 —

10:00 —

11:00 —

Sketch of the Day:

Biggest Limiting Factor:

Aha! Moment:

Observations:

date _____

DAILY GOALS

Faith
time _____ duration _____

Action Items: _____

_____

Notes: _____

Family
time _____ duration _____

Action Items: _____

_____

Notes: _____

Finances
time _____ duration _____

Action Items: _____

_____

Notes: _____

Friends
time _____ duration _____

Action Items: _____

_____

Notes: _____

Fitness
time _____ duration _____

Action Items: _____

_____

Notes: _____

Fun
time _____ duration _____

Action Items: _____

_____

Notes: _____

SCHEDULE

5:00 —

6:00 —

7:00 —

8:00 —

9:00 —

10:00 —

11:00 —

12:00 —

1:00 —

2:00 —

3:00 —

4:00 —

5:00 —

6:00 —

7:00 —

8:00 —

9:00 —

10:00 —

11:00 —

Sketch of the Day:

Biggest Limiting Factor:

Aha! Moment:

Observations:

DAILY GOALS

Faith
time   duration

Action Items: _____

_____

Notes: _____

Family
time   duration

Action Items: _____

_____

Notes: _____

Finances
time   duration

Action Items: _____

_____

Notes: _____

Friends
time   duration

Action Items: _____

_____

Notes: _____

Fitness
time   duration

Action Items: _____

_____

Notes: _____

Fun
time   duration

Action Items: _____

_____

Notes: _____

SCHEDULE

5:00 —

6:00 —

7:00 —

8:00 —

9:00 —

10:00 —

11:00 —

12:00 —

1:00 —

2:00 —

3:00 —

4:00 —

5:00 —

6:00 —

7:00 —

8:00 —

9:00 —

10:00 —

11:00 —

Sketch of the Day:

Biggest Limiting Factor:

Aha! Moment:

Observations:

DAILY GOALS

Faith

time _____ duration _____

Action Items: _____

_____

Notes: _____

Family

time _____ duration _____

Action Items: _____

_____

Notes: _____

Finances

time _____ duration _____

Action Items: _____

_____

Notes: _____

Friends

time _____ duration _____

Action Items: _____

_____

Notes: _____

Fitness

time _____ duration _____

Action Items: _____

_____

Notes: _____

Fun

time _____ duration _____

Action Items: _____

_____

Notes: _____

SCHEDULE

5:00 —

6:00 —

7:00 —

8:00 —

9:00 —

10:00 —

11:00 —

12:00 —

1:00 —

2:00 —

3:00 —

4:00 —

5:00 —

6:00 —

7:00 —

8:00 —

9:00 —

10:00 —

11:00 —

Sketch of the Day:

Biggest Limiting Factor:

Aha! Moment:

Observations:

date _____

DAILY GOALS

Faith
time _____   duration _____

Action Items: _____

_____

Notes: _____

Family
time _____   duration _____

Action Items: _____

_____

Notes: _____

Finances
time _____   duration _____

Action Items: _____

_____

Notes: _____

Friends
time _____   duration _____

Action Items: _____

_____

Notes: _____

Fitness
time _____   duration _____

Action Items: _____

_____

Notes: _____

Fun
time _____   duration _____

Action Items: _____

_____

Notes: _____

SCHEDULE

5:00 —

6:00 —

7:00 —

8:00 —

9:00 —

10:00 —

11:00 —

12:00 —

1:00 —

2:00 —

3:00 —

4:00 —

5:00 —

6:00 —

7:00 —

8:00 —

9:00 —

10:00 —

11:00 —

Sketch of the Day:

Biggest Limiting Factor:

Aha! Moment:

Observations:

date _____

DAILY GOALS

Faith
time _____ duration _____

Action Items: _____

_____

Notes: _____

Family
time _____ duration _____

Action Items: _____

_____

Notes: _____

Finances
time _____ duration _____

Action Items: _____

_____

Notes: _____

Friends
time _____ duration _____

Action Items: _____

_____

Notes: _____

Fitness
time _____ duration _____

Action Items: _____

_____

Notes: _____

Fun
time _____ duration _____

Action Items: _____

_____

Notes: _____

SCHEDULE

5:00 —
6:00 —
7:00 —
8:00 —
9:00 —
10:00 —
11:00 —
12:00 —
1:00 —
2:00 —
3:00 —
4:00 —
5:00 —
6:00 —
7:00 —
8:00 —
9:00 —
10:00 —
11:00 —

Sketch of the Day:

Biggest Limiting Factor:

Aha! Moment:

Observations:

DAILY GOALS

Faith
time   *duration*

Action Items: _____

_____

Notes: _____

Family
time   *duration*

Action Items: _____

_____

Notes: _____

Finances
time   *duration*

Action Items: _____

_____

Notes: _____

Friends
time   *duration*

Action Items: _____

_____

Notes: _____

Fitness
time   *duration*

Action Items: _____

_____

Notes: _____

Fun
time   *duration*

Action Items: _____

_____

Notes: _____

SCHEDULE

5:00 —

6:00 —

7:00 —

8:00 —

9:00 —

10:00 —

11:00 —

12:00 —

1:00 —

2:00 —

3:00 —

4:00 —

5:00 —

6:00 —

7:00 —

8:00 —

9:00 —

10:00 —

11:00 —

Sketch of the Day:

Biggest Limiting Factor:

Aha! Moment:

Observations:

date _____

DAILY GOALS

Faith   time �   duration ▧
Action Items: _____
_____
Notes: _____

Family   time ▧   duration ▧
Action Items: _____
_____
Notes: _____

Finances   time ▧   duration ▧
Action Items: _____
_____
Notes: _____

Friends   time ▧   duration ▧
Action Items: _____
_____
Notes: _____

Fitness   time ▧   duration ▧
Action Items: _____
_____
Notes: _____

Fun   time ▧   duration ▧
Action Items: _____
_____
Notes: _____

SCHEDULE

5:00 —

6:00 —

7:00 —

8:00 —

9:00 —

10:00 —

11:00 —

12:00 —

1:00 —

2:00 —

3:00 —

4:00 —

5:00 —

6:00 —

7:00 —

8:00 —

9:00 —

10:00 —

11:00 —

Sketch of the Day:

Biggest Limiting Factor:

Aha! Moment:

Observations:

DAILY GOALS

Faith   *time*   *duration*

Action Items: _____

_____

Notes: _____

Family   *time*   *duration*

Action Items: _____

_____

Notes: _____

Finances   *time*   *duration*

Action Items: _____

_____

Notes: _____

Friends   *time*   *duration*

Action Items: _____

_____

Notes: _____

Fitness   *time*   *duration*

Action Items: _____

_____

Notes: _____

Fun   *time*   *duration*

Action Items: _____

_____

Notes: _____

SCHEDULE

5:00 —

6:00 —

7:00 —

8:00 —

9:00 —

10:00 —

11:00 —

12:00 —

1:00 —

2:00 —

3:00 —

4:00 —

5:00 —

6:00 —

7:00 —

8:00 —

9:00 —

10:00 —

11:00 —

Sketch of the Day:

Biggest Limiting Factor:

Aha! Moment:

Observations:

date _____

DAILY GOALS

Faith
time _____ duration _____
Action Items: _____
_____
Notes: _____

Family
time _____ duration _____
Action Items: _____
_____
Notes: _____

Finances
time _____ duration _____
Action Items: _____
_____
Notes: _____

Friends
time _____ duration _____
Action Items: _____
_____
Notes: _____

Fitness
time _____ duration _____
Action Items: _____
_____
Notes: _____

Fun
time _____ duration _____
Action Items: _____
_____
Notes: _____

SCHEDULE

5:00 —

6:00 —

7:00 —

8:00 —

9:00 —

10:00 —

11:00 —

12:00 —

1:00 —

2:00 —

3:00 —

4:00 —

5:00 —

6:00 —

7:00 —

8:00 —

9:00 —

10:00 —

11:00 —

Sketch of the Day:

Biggest Limiting Factor:

Aha! Moment:

Observations:

date _____

DAILY GOALS

Faith
Action Items: _____
_____
Notes: _____

time [   ]   duration [   ]

Family
Action Items: _____
_____
Notes: _____

time [   ]   duration [   ]

Finances
Action Items: _____
_____
Notes: _____

time [   ]   duration [   ]

Friends
Action Items: _____
_____
Notes: _____

time [   ]   duration [   ]

Fitness
Action Items: _____
_____
Notes: _____

time [   ]   duration [   ]

Fun
Action Items: _____
_____
Notes: _____

time [   ]   duration [   ]

SCHEDULE

5:00 —

6:00 —

7:00 —

8:00 —

9:00 —

10:00 —

11:00 —

12:00 —

1:00 —

2:00 —

3:00 —

4:00 —

5:00 —

6:00 —

7:00 —

8:00 —

9:00 —

10:00 —

11:00 —

Sketch of the Day:

Biggest Limiting Factor:

Aha! Moment:

Observations:

date _____

DAILY GOALS

Faith
time   duration

Action Items: _____

_____

Notes: _____

Family
time   duration

Action Items: _____

_____

Notes: _____

Finances
time   duration

Action Items: _____

_____

Notes: _____

Friends
time   duration

Action Items: _____

_____

Notes: _____

Fitness
time   duration

Action Items: _____

_____

Notes: _____

Fun
time   duration

Action Items: _____

_____

Notes: _____

SCHEDULE

5:00 —

6:00 —

7:00 —

8:00 —

9:00 —

10:00 —

11:00 —

12:00 —

1:00 —

2:00 —

3:00 —

4:00 —

5:00 —

6:00 —

7:00 —

8:00 —

9:00 —

10:00 —

11:00 —

Sketch of the Day:

Biggest Limiting Factor:

Aha! Moment:

Observations:

date _____

DAILY GOALS

Faith
time _____ duration _____
Action Items: _____
_____
Notes: _____

Family
time _____ duration _____
Action Items: _____
_____
Notes: _____

Finances
time _____ duration _____
Action Items: _____
_____
Notes: _____

Friends
time _____ duration _____
Action Items: _____
_____
Notes: _____

Fitness
time _____ duration _____
Action Items: _____
_____
Notes: _____

Fun
time _____ duration _____
Action Items: _____
_____
Notes: _____

SCHEDULE

5:00 —

6:00 —

7:00 —

8:00 —

9:00 —

10:00 —

11:00 —

12:00 —

1:00 —

2:00 —

3:00 —

4:00 —

5:00 —

6:00 —

7:00 —

8:00 —

9:00 —

10:00 —

11:00 —

Sketch of the Day:

Biggest Limiting Factor:

Aha! Moment:

Observations:

date _____

DAILY GOALS

Faith   time   duration

Action Items: _____

_____

Notes: _____

Family   time   duration

Action Items: _____

_____

Notes: _____

Finances   time   duration

Action Items: _____

_____

Notes: _____

Friends   time   duration

Action Items: _____

_____

Notes: _____

Fitness   time   duration

Action Items: _____

_____

Notes: _____

Fun   time   duration

Action Items: _____

_____

Notes: _____

SCHEDULE

5:00 —

6:00 —

7:00 —

8:00 —

9:00 —

10:00 —

11:00 —

12:00 —

1:00 —

2:00 —

3:00 —

4:00 —

5:00 —

6:00 —

7:00 —

8:00 —

9:00 —

10:00 —

11:00 —

Sketch of the Day:

Biggest Limiting Factor:

Aha! Moment:

Observations:

date _____

DAILY GOALS

Faith
time _____   *duration* _____

Action Items: _____

_____

Notes: _____

Family
time _____   *duration* _____

Action Items: _____

_____

Notes: _____

Finances
time _____   *duration* _____

Action Items: _____

_____

Notes: _____

Friends
time _____   *duration* _____

Action Items: _____

_____

Notes: _____

Fitness
time _____   *duration* _____

Action Items: _____

_____

Notes: _____

Fun
time _____   *duration* _____

Action Items: _____

_____

Notes: _____

SCHEDULE

5:00 —
6:00 —
7:00 —
8:00 —
9:00 —
10:00 —
11:00 —
12:00 —
1:00 —
2:00 —
3:00 —
4:00 —
5:00 —
6:00 —
7:00 —
8:00 —
9:00 —
10:00 —
11:00 —

Sketch of the Day:

Biggest Limiting Factor:

Aha! Moment:

Observations:

DAILY GOALS

Faith
time ░░░░░░░░ duration ░░░░░░░░

Action Items: _____

_____

Notes: _____

Family
time ░░░░░░░░ duration ░░░░░░░░

Action Items: _____

_____

Notes: _____

Finances
time ░░░░░░░░ duration ░░░░░░░░

Action Items: _____

_____

Notes: _____

Friends
time ░░░░░░░░ duration ░░░░░░░░

Action Items: _____

_____

Notes: _____

Fitness
time ░░░░░░░░ duration ░░░░░░░░

Action Items: _____

_____

Notes: _____

Fun
time ░░░░░░░░ duration ░░░░░░░░

Action Items: _____

_____

Notes: _____

SCHEDULE

5:00 —

6:00 —

7:00 —

8:00 —

9:00 —

10:00 —

11:00 —

12:00 —

1:00 —

2:00 —

3:00 —

4:00 —

5:00 —

6:00 —

7:00 —

8:00 —

9:00 —

10:00 —

11:00 —

Sketch of the Day: —————

Biggest Limiting Factor:

Aha! Moment:

Observations:

DAILY GOALS

Faith
time _____   duration _____

Action Items: _____

_____

Notes: _____

Family
time _____   duration _____

Action Items: _____

_____

Notes: _____

Finances
time _____   duration _____

Action Items: _____

_____

Notes: _____

Friends
time _____   duration _____

Action Items: _____

_____

Notes: _____

Fitness
time _____   duration _____

Action Items: _____

_____

Notes: _____

Fun
time _____   duration _____

Action Items: _____

_____

Notes: _____

SCHEDULE

5:00 —

6:00 —

7:00 —

8:00 —

9:00 —

10:00 —

11:00 —

12:00 —

1:00 —

2:00 —

3:00 —

4:00 —

5:00 —

6:00 —

7:00 —

8:00 —

9:00 —

10:00 —

11:00 —

Sketch of the Day:

Biggest Limiting Factor:

Aha! Moment:

Observations:

date _____

DAILY GOALS

Faith
time _____ duration _____

Action Items: _____

_____

Notes: _____

Family
time _____ duration _____

Action Items: _____

_____

Notes: _____

Finances
time _____ duration _____

Action Items: _____

_____

Notes: _____

Friends
time _____ duration _____

Action Items: _____

_____

Notes: _____

Fitness
time _____ duration _____

Action Items: _____

_____

Notes: _____

Fun
time _____ duration _____

Action Items: _____

_____

Notes: _____

SCHEDULE

5:00 —

6:00 —

7:00 —

8:00 —

9:00 —

10:00 —

11:00 —

12:00 —

1:00 —

2:00 —

3:00 —

4:00 —

5:00 —

6:00 —

7:00 —

8:00 —

9:00 —

10:00 —

11:00 —

Sketch of the Day:

Biggest Limiting Factor:

Aha! Moment:

Observations:

DAILY GOALS

Faith
time   duration

Action Items: _____

_____

Notes: _____

Family
time   duration

Action Items: _____

_____

Notes: _____

Finances
time   duration

Action Items: _____

_____

Notes: _____

Friends
time   duration

Action Items: _____

_____

Notes: _____

Fitness
time   duration

Action Items: _____

_____

Notes: _____

Fun
time   duration

Action Items: _____

_____

Notes: _____

SCHEDULE

5:00 —

6:00 —

7:00 —

8:00 —

9:00 —

10:00 —

11:00 —

12:00 —

1:00 —

2:00 —

3:00 —

4:00 —

5:00 —

6:00 —

7:00 —

8:00 —

9:00 —

10:00 —

11:00 —

Sketch of the Day:

Biggest Limiting Factor:

Aha! Moment:

Observations:

DAILY GOALS

Faith

time _____ duration _____

Action Items: _____

_____

Notes: _____

Family

time _____ duration _____

Action Items: _____

_____

Notes: _____

Finances

time _____ duration _____

Action Items: _____

_____

Notes: _____

Friends

time _____ duration _____

Action Items: _____

_____

Notes: _____

Fitness

time _____ duration _____

Action Items: _____

_____

Notes: _____

Fun

time _____ duration _____

Action Items: _____

_____

Notes: _____

SCHEDULE

5:00 —

6:00 —

7:00 —

8:00 —

9:00 —

10:00 —

11:00 —

12:00 —

1:00 —

2:00 —

3:00 —

4:00 —

5:00 —

6:00 —

7:00 —

8:00 —

9:00 —

10:00 —

11:00 —

Sketch of the Day:

Biggest Limiting Factor:

Aha! Moment:

Observations:

DAILY GOALS

Faith
time   duration

Action Items: _____

_____

Notes: _____

Family
time   duration

Action Items: _____

_____

Notes: _____

Finances
time   duration

Action Items: _____

_____

Notes: _____

Friends
time   duration

Action Items: _____

_____

Notes: _____

Fitness
time   duration

Action Items: _____

_____

Notes: _____

Fun
time   duration

Action Items: _____

_____

Notes: _____

SCHEDULE

5:00 —
6:00 —
7:00 —
8:00 —
9:00 —
10:00 —
11:00 —
12:00 —
1:00 —
2:00 —
3:00 —
4:00 —
5:00 —
6:00 —
7:00 —
8:00 —
9:00 —
10:00 —
11:00 —

Sketch of the Day:

Biggest Limiting Factor:

Aha! Moment:

Observations:

date _____

DAILY GOALS

Faith   time _____ duration _____

Action Items: _____

_____

Notes: _____

Family   time _____ duration _____

Action Items: _____

_____

Notes: _____

Finances   time _____ duration _____

Action Items: _____

_____

Notes: _____

Friends   time _____ duration _____

Action Items: _____

_____

Notes: _____

Fitness   time _____ duration _____

Action Items: _____

_____

Notes: _____

Fun   time _____ duration _____

Action Items: _____

_____

Notes: _____

SCHEDULE

5:00 —

6:00 —

7:00 —

8:00 —

9:00 —

10:00 —

11:00 —

12:00 —

1:00 —

2:00 —

3:00 —

4:00 —

5:00 —

6:00 —

7:00 —

8:00 —

9:00 —

10:00 —

11:00 —

Sketch of the Day: ——————

Biggest Limiting Factor:

Aha! Moment:

Observations:

DAILY GOALS

Faith
time   duration

Action Items: _____

_____

Notes: _____

Family
time   duration

Action Items: _____

_____

Notes: _____

Finances
time   duration

Action Items: _____

_____

Notes: _____

Friends
time   duration

Action Items: _____

_____

Notes: _____

Fitness
time   duration

Action Items: _____

_____

Notes: _____

Fun
time   duration

Action Items: _____

_____

Notes: _____

SCHEDULE

5:00 —

6:00 —

7:00 —

8:00 —

9:00 —

10:00 —

11:00 —

12:00 —

1:00 —

2:00 —

3:00 —

4:00 —

5:00 —

6:00 —

7:00 —

8:00 —

9:00 —

10:00 —

11:00 —

Sketch of the Day:

Biggest Limiting Factor:

Aha! Moment:

Observations:

date _____

DAILY GOALS

Faith
time   duration

Action Items: _____

_____

Notes: _____

Family
time   duration

Action Items: _____

_____

Notes: _____

Finances
time   duration

Action Items: _____

_____

Notes: _____

Friends
time   duration

Action Items: _____

_____

Notes: _____

Fitness
time   duration

Action Items: _____

_____

Notes: _____

Fun
time   duration

Action Items: _____

_____

Notes: _____

SCHEDULE

5:00 —

6:00 —

7:00 —

8:00 —

9:00 —

10:00 —

11:00 —

12:00 —

1:00 —

2:00 —

3:00 —

4:00 —

5:00 —

6:00 —

7:00 —

8:00 —

9:00 —

10:00 —

11:00 —

Sketch of the Day:

Biggest Limiting Factor:

Aha! Moment:

Observations:

DAILY GOALS

Faith

time _____ duration _____

Action Items: _____

_____

Notes: _____

Family

time _____ duration _____

Action Items: _____

_____

Notes: _____

Finances

time _____ duration _____

Action Items: _____

_____

Notes: _____

Friends

time _____ duration _____

Action Items: _____

_____

Notes: _____

Fitness

time _____ duration _____

Action Items: _____

_____

Notes: _____

Fun

time _____ duration _____

Action Items: _____

_____

Notes: _____

SCHEDULE

5:00 —

6:00 —

7:00 —

8:00 —

9:00 —

10:00 —

11:00 —

12:00 —

1:00 —

2:00 —

3:00 —

4:00 —

5:00 —

6:00 —

7:00 —

8:00 —

9:00 —

10:00 —

11:00 —

Sketch of the Day:

Biggest Limiting Factor:

Aha! Moment:

Observations:

DAILY GOALS

Faith
time _____   duration _____

Action Items: _____

_____

Notes: _____

Family
time _____   duration _____

Action Items: _____

_____

Notes: _____

Finances
time _____   duration _____

Action Items: _____

_____

Notes: _____

Friends
time _____   duration _____

Action Items: _____

_____

Notes: _____

Fitness
time _____   duration _____

Action Items: _____

_____

Notes: _____

Fun
time _____   duration _____

Action Items: _____

_____

Notes: _____

SCHEDULE

5:00 —

6:00 —

7:00 —

8:00 —

9:00 —

10:00 —

11:00 —

12:00 —

1:00 —

2:00 —

3:00 —

4:00 —

5:00 —

6:00 —

7:00 —

8:00 —

9:00 —

10:00 —

11:00 —

Sketch of the Day:

Biggest Limiting Factor:

Aha! Moment:

Observations:

date _____

DAILY GOALS

Faith
time   duration

Action Items: _____

_____

Notes: _____

Family
time   duration

Action Items: _____

_____

Notes: _____

Finances
time   duration

Action Items: _____

_____

Notes: _____

Friends
time   duration

Action Items: _____

_____

Notes: _____

Fitness
time   duration

Action Items: _____

_____

Notes: _____

Fun
time   duration

Action Items: _____

_____

Notes: _____

SCHEDULE

5:00 —

6:00 —

7:00 —

8:00 —

9:00 —

10:00 —

11:00 —

12:00 —

1:00 —

2:00 —

3:00 —

4:00 —

5:00 —

6:00 —

7:00 —

8:00 —

9:00 —

10:00 —

11:00 —

Sketch of the Day:

Biggest Limiting Factor:

Aha! Moment:

Observations:

DAILY GOALS

Faith
time   duration

Action Items: _____

_____

Notes: _____

Family
time   duration

Action Items: _____

_____

Notes: _____

Finances
time   duration

Action Items: _____

_____

Notes: _____

Friends
time   duration

Action Items: _____

_____

Notes: _____

Fitness
time   duration

Action Items: _____

_____

Notes: _____

Fun
time   duration

Action Items: _____

_____

Notes: _____

SCHEDULE

5:00 —

6:00 —

7:00 —

8:00 —

9:00 —

10:00 —

11:00 —

12:00 —

1:00 —

2:00 —

3:00 —

4:00 —

5:00 —

6:00 —

7:00 —

8:00 —

9:00 —

10:00 —

11:00 —

Sketch of the Day:

Biggest Limiting Factor:

Aha! Moment:

Observations:

date _____

DAILY GOALS

Faith
time _____ duration _____

Action Items: _____

_____

Notes: _____

Family
time _____ duration _____

Action Items: _____

_____

Notes: _____

Finances
time _____ duration _____

Action Items: _____

_____

Notes: _____

Friends
time _____ duration _____

Action Items: _____

_____

Notes: _____

Fitness
time _____ duration _____

Action Items: _____

_____

Notes: _____

Fun
time _____ duration _____

Action Items: _____

_____

Notes: _____

SCHEDULE

5:00 —

6:00 —

7:00 —

8:00 —

9:00 —

10:00 —

11:00 —

12:00 —

1:00 —

2:00 —

3:00 —

4:00 —

5:00 —

6:00 —

7:00 —

8:00 —

9:00 —

10:00 —

11:00 —

Sketch of the Day:

Biggest Limiting Factor:

Aha! Moment:

Observations:

DAILY GOALS

Faith
time   duration

Action Items: _____

_____

Notes: _____

Family
time   duration

Action Items: _____

_____

Notes: _____

Finances
time   duration

Action Items: _____

_____

Notes: _____

Friends
time   duration

Action Items: _____

_____

Notes: _____

Fitness
time   duration

Action Items: _____

_____

Notes: _____

Fun
time   duration

Action Items: _____

_____

Notes: _____

SCHEDULE

5:00 —

6:00 —

7:00 —

8:00 —

9:00 —

10:00 —

11:00 —

12:00 —

1:00 —

2:00 —

3:00 —

4:00 —

5:00 —

6:00 —

7:00 —

8:00 —

9:00 —

10:00 —

11:00 —

Sketch of the Day:

Biggest Limiting Factor:

Aha! Moment:

Observations:

date _____

DAILY GOALS

Faith
time _____ duration _____

Action Items: _____

_____

Notes: _____

Family
time _____ duration _____

Action Items: _____

_____

Notes: _____

Finances
time _____ duration _____

Action Items: _____

_____

Notes: _____

Friends
time _____ duration _____

Action Items: _____

_____

Notes: _____

Fitness
time _____ duration _____

Action Items: _____

_____

Notes: _____

Fun
time _____ duration _____

Action Items: _____

_____

Notes: _____

SCHEDULE

5:00 —

6:00 —

7:00 —

8:00 —

9:00 —

10:00 —

11:00 —

12:00 —

1:00 —

2:00 —

3:00 —

4:00 —

5:00 —

6:00 —

7:00 —

8:00 —

9:00 —

10:00 —

11:00 —

Sketch of the Day:

Biggest Limiting Factor:

Aha! Moment:

Observations:

DAILY GOALS

Faith
time _____ duration _____

Action Items: _____

_____

Notes: _____

Family
time _____ duration _____

Action Items: _____

_____

Notes: _____

Finances
time _____ duration _____

Action Items: _____

_____

Notes: _____

Friends
time _____ duration _____

Action Items: _____

_____

Notes: _____

Fitness
time _____ duration _____

Action Items: _____

_____

Notes: _____

Fun
time _____ duration _____

Action Items: _____

_____

Notes: _____

SCHEDULE

5:00 —

6:00 —

7:00 —

8:00 —

9:00 —

10:00 —

11:00 —

12:00 —

1:00 —

2:00 —

3:00 —

4:00 —

5:00 —

6:00 —

7:00 —

8:00 —

9:00 —

10:00 —

11:00 —

Sketch of the Day:

Biggest Limiting Factor:

Aha! Moment:

Observations:

date _____

DAILY GOALS

Faith   time   duration

Action Items: _____

_____

Notes: _____

Family   time   duration

Action Items: _____

_____

Notes: _____

Finances   time   duration

Action Items: _____

_____

Notes: _____

Friends   time   duration

Action Items: _____

_____

Notes: _____

Fitness   time   duration

Action Items: _____

_____

Notes: _____

Fun   time   duration

Action Items: _____

_____

Notes: _____

SCHEDULE

5:00 —
6:00 —
7:00 —
8:00 —
9:00 —
10:00 —
11:00 —
12:00 —
1:00 —
2:00 —
3:00 —
4:00 —
5:00 —
6:00 —
7:00 —
8:00 —
9:00 —
10:00 —
11:00 —

Sketch of the Day:

Biggest Limiting Factor:

Aha! Moment:

Observations:

date _____

DAILY GOALS

Faith   time ▓▓▓▓▓▓▓   duration ▓▓▓▓▓▓▓

Action Items: _____

_____

Notes: _____

Family   time ▓▓▓▓▓▓▓   duration ▓▓▓▓▓▓▓

Action Items: _____

_____

Notes: _____

Finances   time ▓▓▓▓▓▓▓   duration ▓▓▓▓▓▓▓

Action Items: _____

_____

Notes: _____

Friends   time ▓▓▓▓▓▓▓   duration ▓▓▓▓▓▓▓

Action Items: _____

_____

Notes: _____

Fitness   time ▓▓▓▓▓▓▓   duration ▓▓▓▓▓▓▓

Action Items: _____

_____

Notes: _____

Fun   time ▓▓▓▓▓▓▓   duration ▓▓▓▓▓▓▓

Action Items: _____

_____

Notes: _____

SCHEDULE

5:00 —

6:00 —

7:00 —

8:00 —

9:00 —

10:00 —

11:00 —

12:00 —

1:00 —

2:00 —

3:00 —

4:00 —

5:00 —

6:00 —

7:00 —

8:00 —

9:00 —

10:00 —

11:00 —

Sketch of the Day:

Biggest Limiting Factor:

Aha! Moment:

Observations:

DAILY GOALS

Faith

time   *duration*

Action Items: _____

_____

Notes: _____

Family

time   *duration*

Action Items: _____

_____

Notes: _____

Finances

time   *duration*

Action Items: _____

_____

Notes: _____

Friends

time   *duration*

Action Items: _____

_____

Notes: _____

Fitness

time   *duration*

Action Items: _____

_____

Notes: _____

Fun

time   *duration*

Action Items: _____

_____

Notes: _____

SCHEDULE

5:00 —

6:00 —

7:00 —

8:00 —

9:00 —

10:00 —

11:00 —

12:00 —

1:00 —

2:00 —

3:00 —

4:00 —

5:00 —

6:00 —

7:00 —

8:00 —

9:00 —

10:00 —

11:00 —

Sketch of the Day:

Biggest Limiting Factor:

Aha! Moment:

Observations:

date _____

DAILY GOALS

Faith
time _____ duration _____

Action Items: _____

_____

Notes: _____

Family
time _____ duration _____

Action Items: _____

_____

Notes: _____

Finances
time _____ duration _____

Action Items: _____

_____

Notes: _____

Friends
time _____ duration _____

Action Items: _____

_____

Notes: _____

Fitness
time _____ duration _____

Action Items: _____

_____

Notes: _____

Fun
time _____ duration _____

Action Items: _____

_____

Notes: _____

SCHEDULE

5:00 —

6:00 —

7:00 —

8:00 —

9:00 —

10:00 —

11:00 —

12:00 —

1:00 —

2:00 —

3:00 —

4:00 —

5:00 —

6:00 —

7:00 —

8:00 —

9:00 —

10:00 —

11:00 —

Sketch of the Day:

Biggest Limiting Factor:

Aha! Moment:

Observations:

date _____

DAILY GOALS

Faith
time _____ duration _____

Action Items: _____

_____

Notes: _____

Family
time _____ duration _____

Action Items: _____

_____

Notes: _____

Finances
time _____ duration _____

Action Items: _____

_____

Notes: _____

Friends
time _____ duration _____

Action Items: _____

_____

Notes: _____

Fitness
time _____ duration _____

Action Items: _____

_____

Notes: _____

Fun
time _____ duration _____

Action Items: _____

_____

Notes: _____

SCHEDULE

5:00 —

6:00 —

7:00 —

8:00 —

9:00 —

10:00 —

11:00 —

12:00 —

1:00 —

2:00 —

3:00 —

4:00 —

5:00 —

6:00 —

7:00 —

8:00 —

9:00 —

10:00 —

11:00 —

Sketch of the Day:

Biggest Limiting Factor:

Aha! Moment:

Observations:

date _____

DAILY GOALS

Faith
time _____ duration _____
Action Items: _____
_____
Notes: _____

Family
time _____ duration _____
Action Items: _____
_____
Notes: _____

Finances
time _____ duration _____
Action Items: _____
_____
Notes: _____

Friends
time _____ duration _____
Action Items: _____
_____
Notes: _____

Fitness
time _____ duration _____
Action Items: _____
_____
Notes: _____

Fun
time _____ duration _____
Action Items: _____
_____
Notes: _____

SCHEDULE

5:00 —

6:00 —

7:00 —

8:00 —

9:00 —

10:00 —

11:00 —

12:00 —

1:00 —

2:00 —

3:00 —

4:00 —

5:00 —

6:00 —

7:00 —

8:00 —

9:00 —

10:00 —

11:00 —

Sketch of the Day:

Biggest Limiting Factor:

Aha! Moment:

Observations:

DAILY GOALS

Faith
time   duration

Action Items: _____

_____

Notes: _____

Family
time   duration

Action Items: _____

_____

Notes: _____

Finances
time   duration

Action Items: _____

_____

Notes: _____

Friends
time   duration

Action Items: _____

_____

Notes: _____

Fitness
time   duration

Action Items: _____

_____

Notes: _____

Fun
time   duration

Action Items: _____

_____

Notes: _____

SCHEDULE

5:00 —

6:00 —

7:00 —

8:00 —

9:00 —

10:00 —

11:00 —

12:00 —

1:00 —

2:00 —

3:00 —

4:00 —

5:00 —

6:00 —

7:00 —

8:00 —

9:00 —

10:00 —

11:00 —

Sketch of the Day:

Biggest Limiting Factor:

Aha! Moment:

Observations:

date _____

DAILY GOALS

Faith
time _____ duration _____

Action Items: _____

_____

Notes: _____

Family
time _____ duration _____

Action Items: _____

_____

Notes: _____

Finances
time _____ duration _____

Action Items: _____

_____

Notes: _____

Friends
time _____ duration _____

Action Items: _____

_____

Notes: _____

Fitness
time _____ duration _____

Action Items: _____

_____

Notes: _____

Fun
time _____ duration _____

Action Items: _____

_____

Notes: _____

SCHEDULE

5:00 —

6:00 —

7:00 —

8:00 —

9:00 —

10:00 —

11:00 —

12:00 —

1:00 —

2:00 —

3:00 —

4:00 —

5:00 —

6:00 —

7:00 —

8:00 —

9:00 —

10:00 —

11:00 —

Sketch of the Day:

Biggest Limiting Factor:

Aha! Moment:

Observations:

date ______________________

DAILY GOALS

Faith
time ______ *duration* ______

Action Items: ______________________

____

Notes: ______________________

Family
time ______ *duration* ______

Action Items: ______________________

____

Notes: ______________________

Finances
time ______ *duration* ______

Action Items: ______________________

____

Notes: ______________________

Friends
time ______ *duration* ______

Action Items: ______________________

____

Notes: ______________________

Fitness
time ______ *duration* ______

Action Items: ______________________

____

Notes: ______________________

Fun
time ______ *duration* ______

Action Items: ______________________

____

Notes: ______________________

SCHEDULE

5:00 —

6:00 —

7:00 —

8:00 —

9:00 —

10:00 —

11:00 —

12:00 —

1:00 —

2:00 —

3:00 —

4:00 —

5:00 —

6:00 —

7:00 —

8:00 —

9:00 —

10:00 —

11:00 —

Sketch of the Day:

Biggest Limiting Factor:

Aha! Moment:

Observations:

DAILY GOALS

Faith
time   duration

Action Items: _____

_____

Notes: _____

Family
time   duration

Action Items: _____

_____

Notes: _____

Finances
time   duration

Action Items: _____

_____

Notes: _____

Friends
time   duration

Action Items: _____

_____

Notes: _____

Fitness
time   duration

Action Items: _____

_____

Notes: _____

Fun
time   duration

Action Items: _____

_____

Notes: _____

SCHEDULE

5:00 —

6:00 —

7:00 —

8:00 —

9:00 —

10:00 —

11:00 —

12:00 —

1:00 —

2:00 —

3:00 —

4:00 —

5:00 —

6:00 —

7:00 —

8:00 —

9:00 —

10:00 —

11:00 —

Sketch of the Day:

Biggest Limiting Factor:

Aha! Moment:

Observations:

date _____

DAILY GOALS

Faith   time _____   duration _____

Action Items: _____

_____

Notes: _____

Family   time _____   duration _____

Action Items: _____

_____

Notes: _____

Finances   time _____   duration _____

Action Items: _____

_____

Notes: _____

Friends   time _____   duration _____

Action Items: _____

_____

Notes: _____

Fitness   time _____   duration _____

Action Items: _____

_____

Notes: _____

Fun   time _____   duration _____

Action Items: _____

_____

Notes: _____

SCHEDULE

5:00 —

6:00 —

7:00 —

8:00 —

9:00 —

10:00 —

11:00 —

12:00 —

1:00 —

2:00 —

3:00 —

4:00 —

5:00 —

6:00 —

7:00 —

8:00 —

9:00 —

10:00 —

11:00 —

Sketch of the Day:

Biggest Limiting Factor:

Aha! Moment:

Observations:

DAILY GOALS

Faith

time _____ *duration* _____

Action Items: _____

_____

Notes: _____

Family

time _____ *duration* _____

Action Items: _____

_____

Notes: _____

Finances

time _____ *duration* _____

Action Items: _____

_____

Notes: _____

Friends

time _____ *duration* _____

Action Items: _____

_____

Notes: _____

Fitness

time _____ *duration* _____

Action Items: _____

_____

Notes: _____

Fun

time _____ *duration* _____

Action Items: _____

_____

Notes: _____

SCHEDULE

5:00 —

6:00 —

7:00 —

8:00 —

9:00 —

10:00 —

11:00 —

12:00 —

1:00 —

2:00 —

3:00 —

4:00 —

5:00 —

6:00 —

7:00 —

8:00 —

9:00 —

10:00 —

11:00 —

Sketch of the Day:

Biggest Limiting Factor:

Aha! Moment:

Observations:

date _____

DAILY GOALS

Faith
time _____   duration _____

Action Items: _____

_____

Notes: _____

Family
time _____   duration _____

Action Items: _____

_____

Notes: _____

Finances
time _____   duration _____

Action Items: _____

_____

Notes: _____

Friends
time _____   duration _____

Action Items: _____

_____

Notes: _____

Fitness
time _____   duration _____

Action Items: _____

_____

Notes: _____

Fun
time _____   duration _____

Action Items: _____

_____

Notes: _____

SCHEDULE

5:00 —

6:00 —

7:00 —

8:00 —

9:00 —

10:00 —

11:00 —

12:00 —

1:00 —

2:00 —

3:00 —

4:00 —

5:00 —

6:00 —

7:00 —

8:00 —

9:00 —

10:00 —

11:00 —

Sketch of the Day:

Biggest Limiting Factor:

Aha! Moment:

Observations:

CHECK OUT OUR OTHER LIFE CHANGING AND MINDSET REARRANGING TITLES

Start Here

NEVER before has entrepreneurship been delivered in an UNFILTERED, real and raw way. This book is NOT for people who want a politically correct and silver-lined happy-go-lucky view of entrepreneurship. That's crap. Supported by case studies and testimonials from entrepreneurs that have grown their businesses all over the planet using these best practice systems, former US Small Business Administration Entrepreneur of the Year, Clay Clark shares the specific action steps for successful business systems, hilarious stories from situations that every entrepreneur faces, and entrepreneurship factoids that are guaranteed to blow your mind.

Jackassery

Learn how to achieve success by vaccinating yourself against the wealth-destroying disease called Jackassery! In this hilarious and unfiltered letter to his younger self, Clay Clark, radio talk show host and 2007 SBA Entrepreneur of the Year, outlines his former Jackassery and the solutions to eradicating it for the greater good of, well, himself. Learn money multiplying tricks like "Stop watching 5 hours of TV a day" and life lessons like "once you say 'with all due respect' you can say anything you want." If Jackassery is holding you or "a friend" back in business (or even just in life), this is the book for you... or, you know... your "friend who needs it."

Thrive

What is an entrepreneur? Basically, an entrepreneur is someone who seeks to solve a problem in the world in exchange for enough monetary compensation to achieve their own personal dreams. THRIVE, by author and Serial Entrepreneur Clay Clark, is a practical guide on how to specifically go from just surviving to thriving. It is great for anyone who is dissatisfied with where they currently are in life. If you have a functional brain and you embrace the truth that entrepreneurship is a viable option to take you from where you are to where you want to be, this book has the power to change your life.

Join The World's Best 2-Day Intensive Business Workshop

Get specific and practical training on how to grow your business!

www.thrive15.com/conference